American Moments

ABDO & Daughters

THE GREAT DEPRESSION

By Cory Gunderson

VISIT US AT
WWW.ABDOPUB.COM

Published by ABDO Publishing Company, 4940 Viking Drive, Suite 622, Edina, Minnesota 55435. Copyright ©2004 by Abdo Consulting Group, Inc. International copyrights reserved in all countries. No part of this book may be reproduced in any form without written permission from the publisher.

Printed in the United States.

Edited by: Melanie A. Howard
Contributing Editor: Tamara L. Britton
Interior Production and Design: Terry Dunham Incorporated
Cover Design: Mighty Media
Photos: Corbis, Library of Congress

Library of Congress Cataloging-in-Publication Data

Gunderson, Cory Gideon.
  The Great Depression / Cory Gunderson.
    p. cm. -- (American moments)
  Includes index.
  ISBN 1-59197-286-8
  1. Depressions--1929--United States--Juvenile literature. 2. Stock Market Crash, 1929--Juvenile literature. 3. United States--Economic conditions--1918-1945--Juvenile literature. 4. New Deal, 1933-1939--Juvenile literature. 5. Europe--Economic conditions--1918-1945--Juvenile literature. [1. Depressions--1929. 2. Stock Market Crash, 1929. 3. United States--Economic conditions--1918-1945. 4. Europe--Economic conditions--1918-1945.] I. Title. II. Series.

HB37171929 .G86 2004
338.5'42'097309043--dc22

2003069307

Contents

The Depression Like No Other 4

A Lesson in Economics 6

The Roaring Twenties 12

The Crash of October 29, 1929 16

A Nation in Debt 20

Worldwide Impact 26

New President, New Deal 30

A Changed Nation 40

Timeline 42

Fast Facts 44

Web Sites 45

Glossary 46

Index 48

American Moments

THE DEPRESSION LIKE NO OTHER

The Great Depression of the 1930s was not the only economic decline in U.S. history. Others occurred in 1873–1879, 1893–1897, 1907–1908, and 1920–1921. But the suffering that gripped American citizens during the Great Depression was so severe that it has been widely accepted as the worst in U.S. history.

During the Great Depression, people lost their homes, farms, and businesses. Many people died from disease and malnutrition. Jobs became scarce, and poverty plagued the nation.

In the early 1930s, the U.S. government decided to take action. It began taking more control of business than it had in the past. By the time the Great Depression ended, the role of government in the economy had forever changed.

Above: *A mother comforts her children after they learn they have lost their home.*

New York police officers help distribute food to needy men and women.

A LESSON IN ECONOMICS

The word *economy* refers to a system that regulates the distribution of goods and services that people use. It is an enormous and complex mechanism that cannot be seen. But it is very real. It is the way a community, region, or country produces, distributes, and consumes its goods and services.

A *good* is a product. Items such as shaving creams, cars, apples, watches, and doorknobs are goods. *Services* are different. A service is something that someone else does for you. Getting a cavity filled is a service. So is an eye exam, a haircut, or a car repair. Most goods and services cost money.

Just as people cannot afford to buy all the goods and services they want, no country is able to produce everything that its citizens want. The problem of having less than we want is called scarcity. Governments, like people, must decide how they will best use the limited resources that they have.

Each place a good or service can be bought and sold is called a market. A farmer's roadside vegetable stand is a market. Although on the Internet, eBay is also a market.

A man sells apples on a busy street corner during the Great Depression.

The stock market is another example of a large market. This is the place where stocks are bought and sold. Stocks are portions of a business that are sold to raise money. The money raised by the sale of stocks allows the business to invest in itself and expand. In return, the buyer of the stock, the stockholder, owns part of the business. If the business makes money, the stockholder will, too. But if the business loses money, a stockholder can lose part or all of his or her investment. This means that there is always a risk when buying stocks.

A *bull market* happens when more stock is being bought than sold. A bull market represents a period of time when investors believe that stock prices will continue to rise. They believe that their investments will keep growing in value.

STOCK EXCHANGE

This photo shows an area of New York that used to be called the Curb Exchange. The Curb Exchange was located on Wall Street and was a place where stock traders gathered to do business. Eventually, the market moved indoors and was renamed the American Stock Exchange.

The opposite stock market condition is a *bear market*. During a bear market, people do not have much faith in the stock market. Investors fear that their stocks will decrease in value. People start selling their stocks because they think that they are going to lose money. Stock prices decrease as people sell their stocks.

Bear markets usually happen when people stop buying goods. Businesses then stop making the products. This means the workers have nothing to make, and they lose their jobs. The economy is in danger when there is less buying and selling because it causes a decrease in production, prices, income, and jobs. It slows down the economy.

Times when the economy slows down are called *recessions*. A recession can lead to a depression, or low point in the economy.

Many people lost their jobs during the Great Depression. In this photo, an employment agency is crowded with men seeking work.

During a depression, there is very little buying or selling, and unemployment is high.

Depressions do not begin or end quickly. They happen slowly over time. It is natural for a country to have depressions and peaks, or economic highs. These usually follow each other in a cycle.

But when a depression is very bad, it can harm an industry, an area, a country, or even the world. Depressions have been known to hit countries following the ends of wars. When wartime spending ceases, it is difficult for the economy to adjust. This is one of the factors that led to the Great Depression.

DID YOU KNOW?

Did you know that it is very uncommon for the economy to stay the same? Usually, it is either going up or down. Ups and downs in the economy happen in business cycles. A business cycle can be shown as a wave, like the one pictured below. This cycle consists of four stages: recession, depression, recovery, and peak.

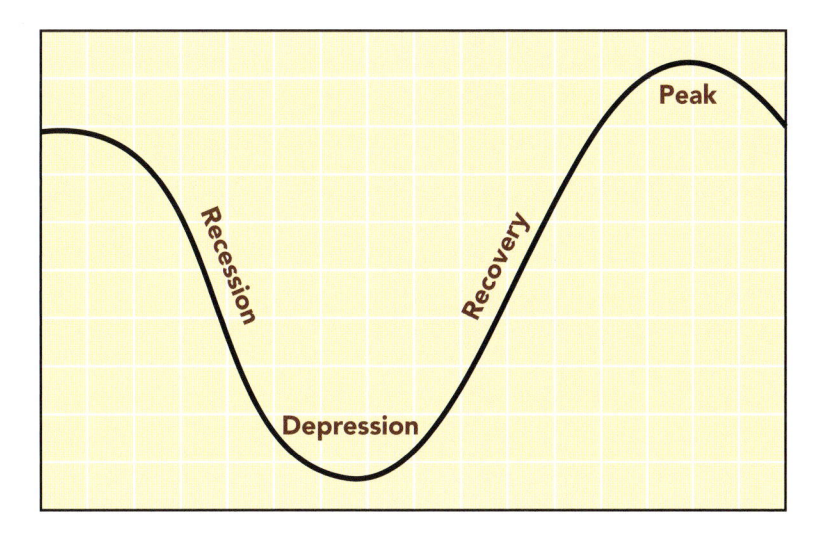

STAGE 1–RECESSION
The downward slope of the wave above represents a recession. Business activity slows down during a recession, which causes the economy to go down.

STAGE 2–DEPRESSION
At the very bottom of the recession is a depression. It covers the time that a recession is at its worst.

STAGE 3–RECOVERY
The upward slope of the wave is called recovery. Recovery happens after a depression or recession and is a period of time when business activity increases. This is also called expansion.

STAGE 4–PEAK
A boom happens at the peak of expansion. The peak, or top of the wave, represents a period of time when the economy is at its best, and business activity is at its highest.

American Moments

THE ROARING TWENTIES

In order to understand the Great Depression, it is important to understand what came before it. World War I had ended in 1918. The United States economy was strong. For this reason, the 1920s are often called the Roaring Twenties. It was a time of prosperity and hope.

During this period, assembly lines were making more goods faster than ever before. This mass production made many items such as washing machines more abundant. Because there were more goods, many of them became more affordable than in previous decades. And those who wanted to buy them didn't have to rely on their savings. Consumers found that many major purchases could now be bought on credit. This meant businesses lent part of the purchase price to customers. Customers eventually would need to pay back the amount.

Before the 1920s, people had avoided going into debt. Debt was seen as an embarrassment. Then the advertising industry became bigger in the 1920s. It began promoting the purchase of goods on credit. Ads in movie theaters and magazines, as well as on the radio, encouraged Americans to buy now and pay later. These campaigns changed the way U.S. citizens regarded debt. By the end of the decade, debt was widely accepted.

Businesses such as car companies started selling goods on credit because it guaranteed that they would have money throughout the year. Some products were only bought at certain times of the year. If businesses sold those goods on credit, then they would have money all year round. That meant that they wouldn't have to lay off their workers during the time of the year when products were not being bought.

Billboards tower over the streets of New York in 1923.

The practice of buying on credit proved to be a boon for businesses. Manufacturing went up more than 60 percent throughout the decade. People started buying products such as cars, radios, vacuum cleaners, and refrigerators. They bought many of these items on credit. Sales in the United States increased through the 1920s. But so did consumer debt.

Many people also used credit to buy stock. Banks loaned people money to invest in the stock market. Hoping to get rich, people rushed to secure these loans. With so many people investing, stock prices went up. The investors created a bull market.

With business owners and investors making so much money, the 1920s became known for its widespread abundance. Most people assumed that the era of prosperity would never end. Few understood how the economy's foundation was actually quite unstable.

Debt rose significantly in the 1920s. But the wages of average workers did not increase enough to cover their debt. Too much consumer credit led to the production of too many goods. Eventually, people could no longer afford to buy what was being produced.

In fact, even though the 1920s was an era of prosperity, the financial gap between the rich and the poor was getting bigger. A healthy economy will usually have a large middle class. This means that a nation's wealth is more evenly distributed. During the 1920s, the middle class started to disappear.

By the end of the decade, the richest 1 percent of families owned about 45 percent of the nation's wealth. This imbalance hurt the economy. Rich people had most of the money, but could only buy so much. The poor and middle class could afford to buy even less.

An economy can only keep going when supply is equal to demand. Unfortunately, the poor and middle class had gotten themselves too far in debt for demand to stay high. The prosperity of the Roaring Twenties could not sustain itself.

The A.W. Bishop Company displays a going out of business sign in the window. The Great Depression forced many store owners out of business.

CALVIN COOLIDGE

Calvin Coolidge served as president during the Roaring Twenties. Coolidge captured the booming spirit of the time when he said, "The chief business of the American people is business."

THE CRASH OF OCTOBER 29, 1929

By 1929, stock prices had risen to four times what they were worth in 1920. As the prices of shares increased, so did the number of people who borrowed money to buy shares. Shares are certificates that show ownership in part of a corporation. Many people saw the stock market as a sure way to increase their money.

All the speculation made the Federal Reserve Board nervous. Borrowing money to invest in the stock market was dangerous. The Federal Reserve Board raised interest rates on loans in 1928 and 1929. It was hoped that by making borrowed money cost more, fewer people would use it in the stock market.

The higher interest rates resulted in less consumer spending. Since fewer people were buying new goods, production began to slow. Businesses started making less money. This made the value of stocks go down. People saw this and started selling their stock.

As more people sold stock, the bull market turned into a bear market. On Thursday, October 24, 1929, the prices of shares plunged. This day became known as Black Thursday.

Share prices dropped again on Monday. Then on Tuesday, October 29, a panic swept over stock market investors. Many more people

Opposite page: *After the stock market plummeted, 400 police were dispatched to protect the financial district.*

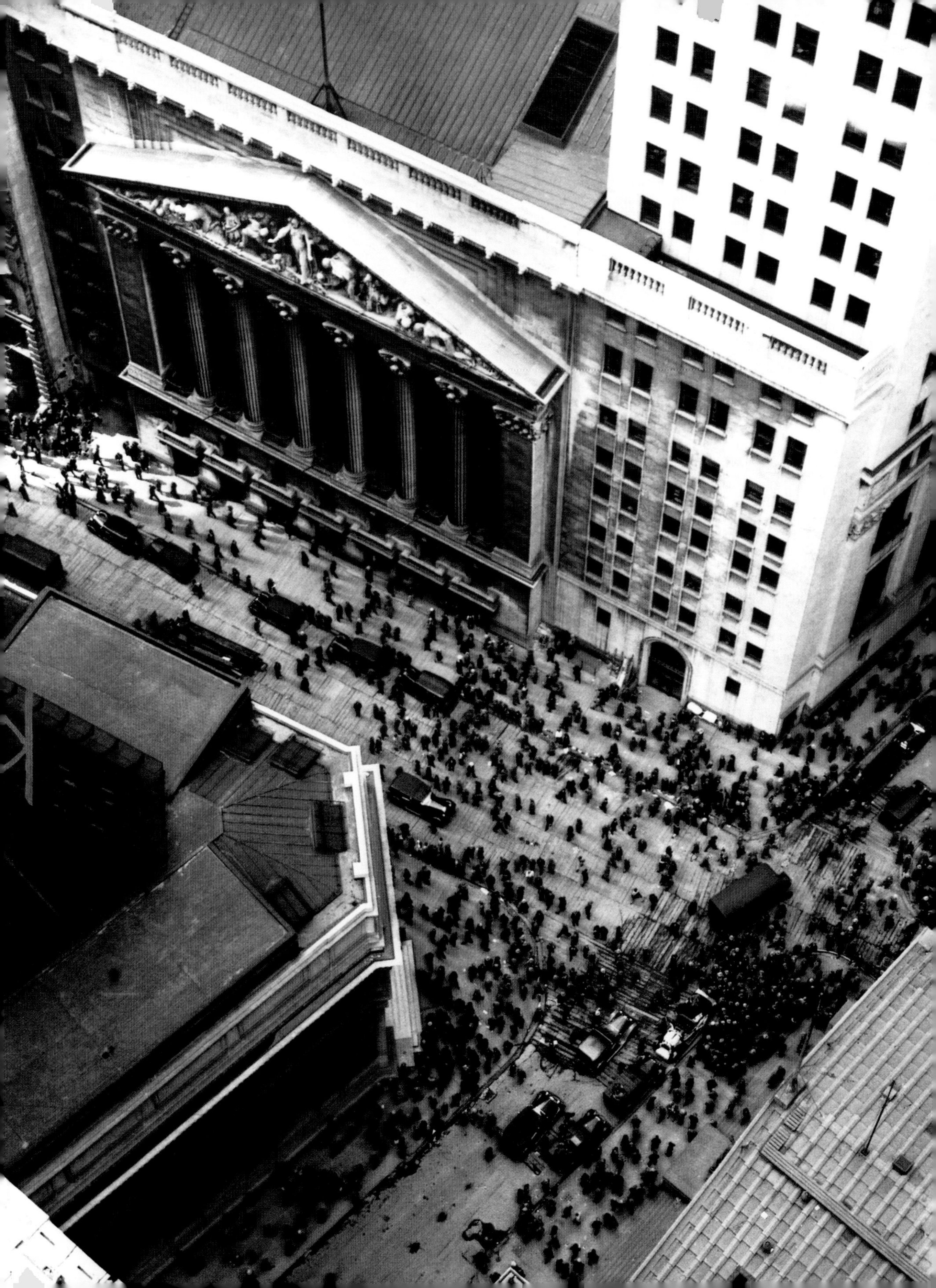

started selling their stocks. They wanted to dump their stocks before the value decreased too much. A record 16,410,030 shares were sold.

The lower demand for shares resulted in an 80 percent decrease in share value. Stocks became almost worthless. October 29, 1929, went down in history as Black Tuesday, the day the stock market collapsed.

FOLLOWING THE STOCK MARKET CRASH OF 1929

Some investors and brokers were so upset by the initial crash that they jumped off ledges of Manhattan skyscrapers. One dejected broker was reportedly held back from jumping by his wife and daughter. After the crash, brokers and bankers were not treated as heroes as they were during the market's heyday. Instead of receiving honorary degrees and prestigious invitations as they once had, brokers and bankers were scrutinized by the public during the Depression. However, contrary to popular belief, not all stocks were worthless. In the weeks following the crash, reliable stocks in companies such as GM and RCA rallied to regain some value.

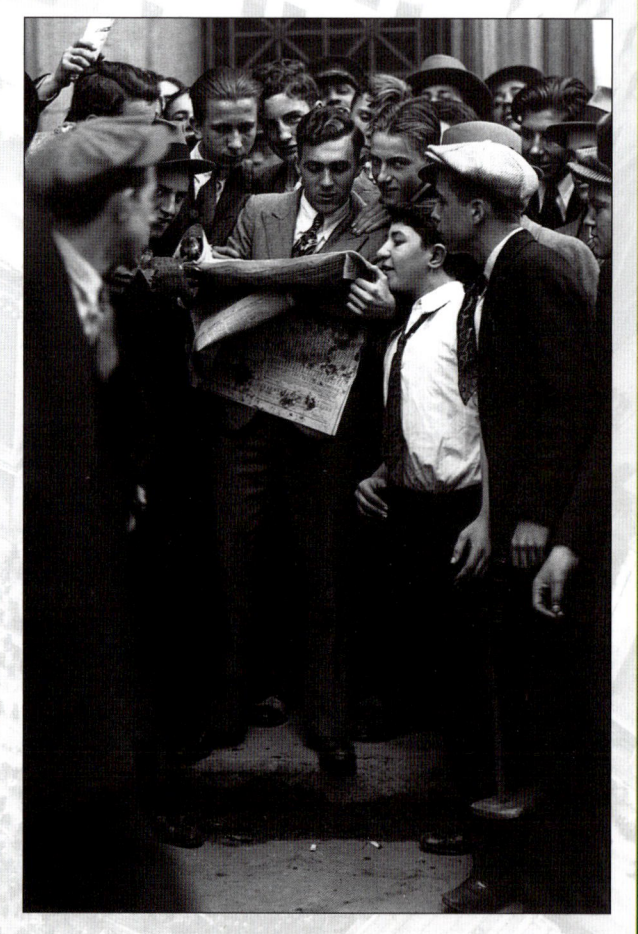

Panic on Wall Street

The newspaper headline from the Broadway Variety on October 30, 1929, the day after the crash

American Moments

A NATION IN DEBT

Following the stock market crash, brokerages asked investors to pay off money that had been borrowed to purchase stocks. Investors flooded the banks to withdraw money to pay the brokerages.

As regular bank customers saw what was happening, they also went to the bank to withdraw their money. Unfortunately, many banks did not have enough money to cover their customers' deposits. They had lent the money to people investing in the stock market.

At that time, money in banks was not federally insured. This meant that if a person's bank went out of business, that person's money was gone. Millions of people lost money. Some lost their entire life savings, either in the stock market or because the banks did not have the money to repay their regular customers.

Between 1930 and 1933, about 9,000 banks went out of business. The closing of the banks affected industry, because there was less money available for borrowing. Less money available to industry meant less production, and less production meant increased unemployment.

By 1933, unemployment reached 25 percent. Those people lucky enough to find a job typically earned 18 percent less than they had before the stock market collapsed.

New Yorkers line up at the American Union Bank only to find that it has closed.

Consumer product prices dropped by 25 percent between 1929 and 1933. The prices of farm products did even worse. They plunged more than 50 percent within the same period. During this time, farmers produced more crops than people could purchase. Farmers lost money, and many could not afford to pay back the money they had borrowed from banks. Many farmers lost their farms.

To make matters even worse for farmers, there was a severe drought throughout the 1930s. Low rainfall, high temperatures, and strong winds gave rise to swarms of invading insects and dust storms on the Great Plains. This affected area became known as the Dust Bowl.

Millions of people fled the Dust Bowl of the Midwest and Southwest because they could not make enough money to live. They headed to the West Coast, where they hoped to find work.

Some did find jobs picking fruit on fertile California farms. But they earned extremely low wages. Migrant families were forced to live in crowded shacks or camp outdoors near the fields where they worked. The constant migration from job to job and town to town caused a lot of stress for the migrant families.

Farmers and urban residents could no longer provide for their families. So, they stood in line for free bread and soup. Some became so desperate they stole to provide their families with food and clothing. Many couldn't handle the stress and embarrassment of this new way of life and committed suicide.

Children from poor families dropped out of school to earn money to support their families. The overall financial situation was so bad that even many lower-middle-class fathers had barely enough money to give their families enough to survive.

The U.S. economy continued to fall throughout the 1930s. And it took the economies of other countries down with it.

Opposite page: *Lines of homeless people wait for shelter.*

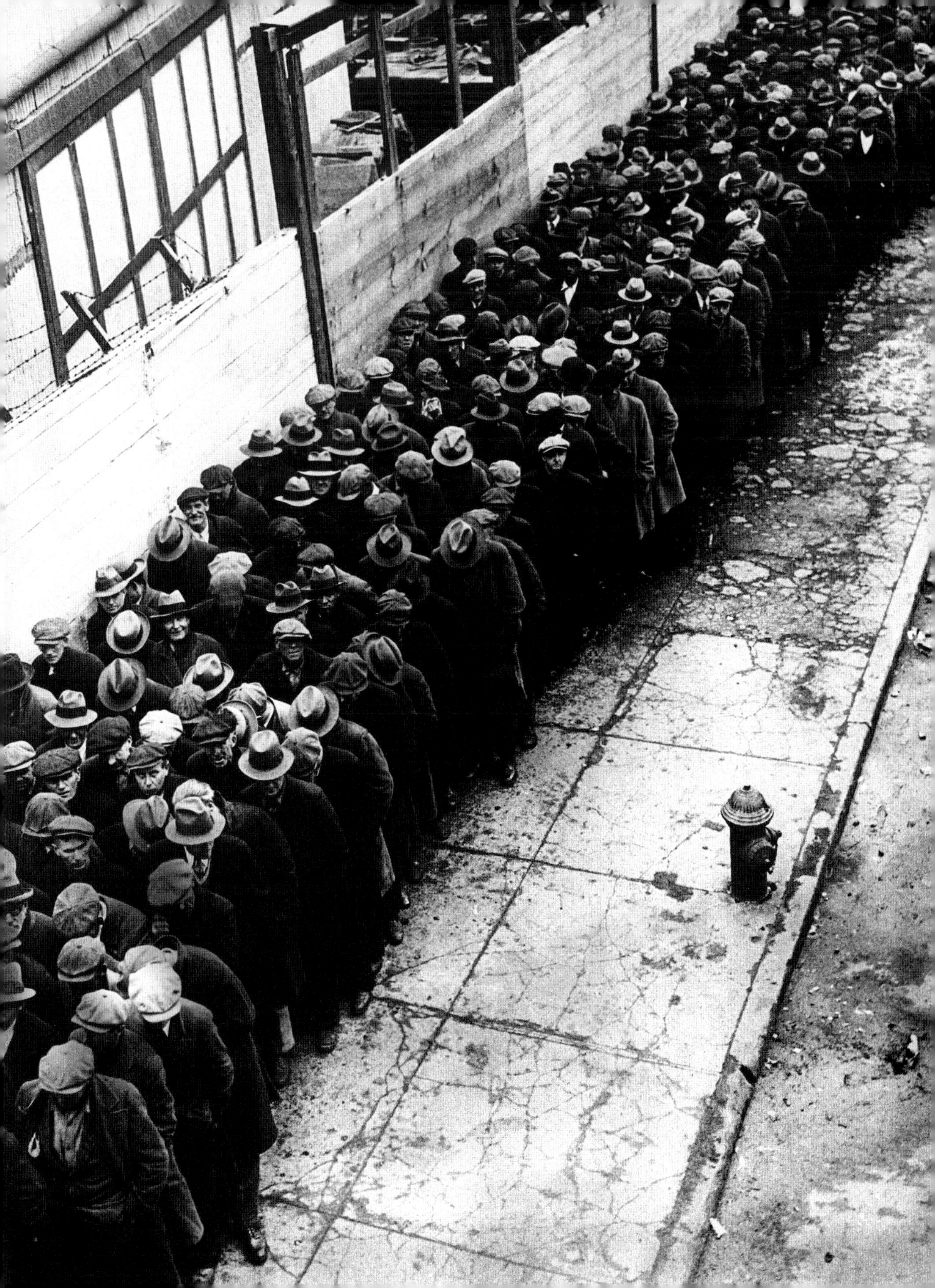

Vernon Evans, a migrant farm worker from South Dakota, stands next to his Model T car which reads, "Oregon or Bust." The Evans family is migrating to Oregon in hopes of improving their lives.

Farmers were having trouble even before the Depression hit. During the 1920s, many farmers struggled because they were producing more goods than they could sell. Prices fell sharply and many farmers went into debt.

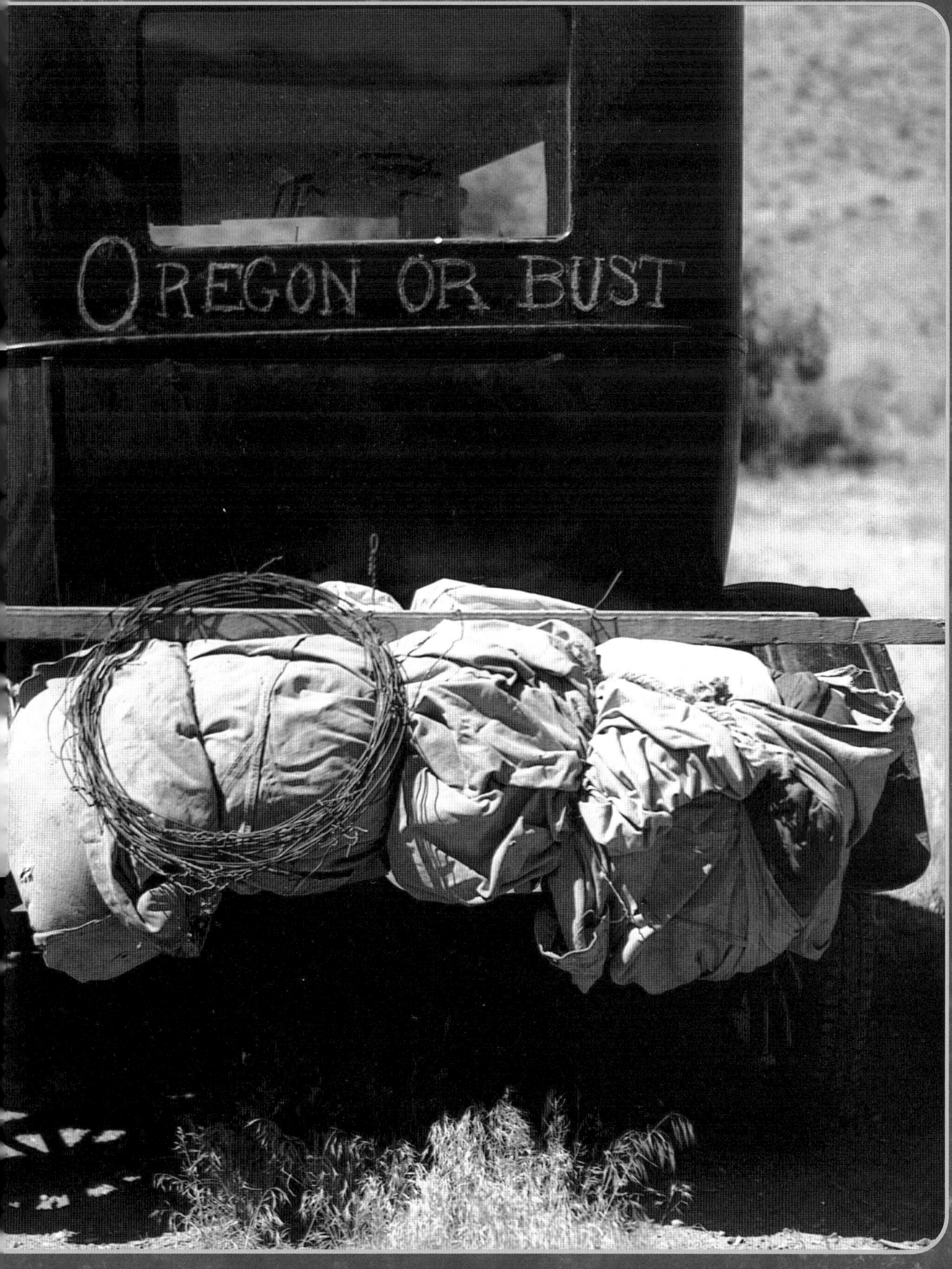
OREGON OR BUST

American Moments

WORLDWIDE IMPACT

Even before the collapse, the world's economic situation was unstable. Many countries that had been involved in World War I were still struggling to pay off their war debts in the 1920s.

The total cost of World War I was over $180 billion. That amount had been financed through the use of loans. The United States had lent money to its allies to help finance the war.

After the war, many European countries had to pay off their loans. But at the same time, they needed money to rebuild because many cities had been badly damaged by fighting. The United States had not been bombed during the war. So the country was in better financial shape than European nations were after the war.

In the decade following World War I, many European countries asked the United States if their debts could be forgiven. At the very least, they wanted the United States to lessen the amount they had to repay. But the U.S. government insisted on being repaid. The government intended to use the money to pay off its own debts.

European countries were forced to borrow more money from U.S. banks to pay back the money they owed to the U.S. government. While the United States was enjoying the great prosperity of the Roaring Twenties, Europe was just starting to recover.

When the Great Depression hit the United States, money became scarcer. The European countries had a harder time getting U.S. bank loans and were unable to make their repayments. The European economy soon followed the U.S. economy into the Great Depression.

To make matters worse, the U.S. Congress decided to pass the Hawley-Smoot Tariff Act in 1930. U.S. president Herbert Hoover signed the act hoping that it would help the U.S. economy. He thought that by charging increased taxes for the goods other countries exported to the United States, more citizens would prefer to buy American-made goods.

Herbert Hoover

Instead, the Hawley-Smoot Tariff Act hurt the U.S. economy. Foreign countries struck back at the United States by increasing taxes on U.S. imports. World trade fell significantly. These actions intensified the Great Depression globally.

The Depression grew severe enough that Germany could not afford to repay the United States in 1931. Other countries struggled with their loans, too. Hoover allowed struggling nations to put off payments for one year. This decision was called the Hoover Moratorium.

While the moratorium helped European nations a little, it was not enough to stop the economic damage the Great Depression was causing. By 1932, there were few opportunities to work in Europe or in the United States. U.S. citizens feared that the hard economic times would never end. They needed a leader who could help end the Great Depression.

Charities and churches set up soup kitchens, as seen here, and bread lines during the Great Depression. In 1933, one in every four workers was unemployed. This was roughly 13 million people.

American Moments

NEW PRESIDENT, NEW DEAL

In the early part of the Great Depression, Hoover thought that each state and community should help its own unemployed citizens. Later it became clear that the unemployed needed more help than either the state or local community could provide. Congress ended up providing financial aid to the states so that they could help the jobless.

Even though Hoover did eventually support other types of assistance, most U.S. citizens felt that it was not enough. Many held him responsible for the Great Depression and called him the "do-nothing president."

Hoover ran for reelection in 1932. U.S. citizens used their voting power to show Hoover that they did not like his leadership. Hoover's Democratic opponent, Franklin D. Roosevelt, won the election by a wide margin. Roosevelt had the support of 42 out of 48 states.

Roosevelt had such widespread support because of the promise he made to the American people. He promised, "I pledge you, I pledge myself, to a new deal for the American people." Roosevelt provided hope to the masses that were starting to lose faith in the government. He assured Americans that he would take action to protect the U.S. economy from future depressions.

Roosevelt's plan to use the government to revive the economy became known as the New Deal. Roosevelt didn't share Hoover's belief that a laissez-faire government policy could correct the depressed economy. He believed that the federal government should take action to correct it.

Franklin D. Roosevelt and Herbert Hoover ride to Roosevelt's inauguration.

Roosevelt's administration was quick to come up with legislation that would help the economy recover. The new laws were designed to bring relief to those in need, and recovery to those who were jobless. Other laws reformed business and government. Roosevelt believed that reforms of business and government were necessary to avoid another severe depression.

On March 6, 1933, Roosevelt announced that there would be a bank holiday until Congress could meet. This was his first project as U.S. president. About three weeks before Roosevelt had become president, nervous depositors had begun rushing to the banks to withdraw their money. These bank customers feared that their banks would close and leave them poor.

This banking crisis threatened to worsen an already severe depression. The closing of all U.S. banks gave the Department of the Treasury time to research every bank's books. Then the Treasury forwarded money to those banks in good financial shape, which allowed them to stay in business.

Those banks that were not in sound financial shape were forced to stay closed until they could improve. Many never reopened. These actions were called for under the Emergency Banking Bill of 1933, which Congress wrote and Roosevelt signed.

Three months later, Roosevelt signed the Glass-Steagall Act. This act established the Federal Deposit Insurance Corporation (FDIC), which guaranteed that people's deposits in national banks were safe. The FDIC insured consumer deposits up to $5,000. This ended the bank crisis because people no longer felt that they had to withdraw their money to keep it safe.

Roosevelt signs the Glass–Steagall Act.

These banking improvements were just the beginning of the changes led by Roosevelt. The president called a special session of Congress on March 5, 1933. Congress convened on March 9. Over the next several months, Roosevelt introduced many important bills to help improve the economy. Congress approved almost all of them. This period of time between March 9 and June 16 became known as the Hundred Days.

New Deal legislation passed during the Hundred Days included the Agricultural Adjustment Act (AAA) and the National Industrial Recovery Act (NIRA). Other legislation created the Civilian Conservation Corps (CCC) and the Tennessee Valley Authority (TVA).

The goal of the AAA recovery effort was to maintain reasonable prices for produce. Because farms were producing too much food for people to buy, the U.S. government paid farmers to destroy some of the livestock and crops that they raised. This helped farmers by making sure that their products would be worth more money. Between 1932 and 1935, farmers' incomes grew by more than 50 percent.

Congress passed the Reforestation Relief Act on March 31, 1933. This act established the CCC. It created work for 250,000 jobless men between the ages of 18 and 25. Workers were paid $30 a month, which equals roughly $333 today. These men built roads and public buildings, and they developed national forests.

The TVA recovery legislation provided even more jobs. The TVA set up a program to build dams and power plants in the Tennessee Valley region. Cheap electricity generated by the dams and power plants benefited many people in the region who had never had electricity. The dams also helped control flooding and made it easier to navigate the rivers in that region.

Some U.S. citizens criticized this relief effort. They felt the created jobs were unnecessary. Still, these jobs improved the U.S. landscape and helped employ more than 2 million people over ten years.

June 16, 1933, was the last day of the Hundred Days. It was on this day that Congress passed the NIRA. This act provided for the establishment of the National Recovery Administration (NRA). The goal of the NRA was to generate more jobs by establishing rules for fair competitive practice in business.

San Francisco schoolchildren form the patriotic blue eagle of the National Recovery Administration.

A sticker for the New Deal National Recovery Administration shows the organization's symbol and slogan.

Under the NRA, businesses were urged to ask their employees to work no more than 40 hours each week. They were also encouraged to pay their workers at least 40¢ an hour. Workers were also granted the right to group together to ask for better working conditions.

The NRA was popular at first. But after a while, businesses began to complain about the government control. Many small businesses felt that the NRA gave big businesses an unfair advantage. By 1935, the NRA was labeled unconstitutional.

Another important act in the New Deal was the Securities Exchange Act of 1934. It was passed almost a year after the Hundred Days on June 6, 1934. The act established the Securities and Exchange Commission (SEC). This commission's job was to watch over stock market deals. The SEC could pursue legal action against those who were not honest in their transactions. This meant more protection for investors.

On January 17, 1935, Roosevelt announced to Congress his long-term goals to provide security for the old, sick, and jobless. This announcement introduced the second phase of Roosevelt's New Deal. Some even called it the "second New Deal."

The "second New Deal" included new legislation such as the Works Progress Administration (WPA). Other legislation included the National Labor Relations Act, the Social Security Act, and the Banking Act of 1935.

The WPA was a project created as part of the Emergency Relief Appropriation Act on April 8, 1935. The goal of the WPA was to provide more government jobs for those without work. Some WPA projects included the construction of schools, roads, and airports. Other projects employed artists to make things such as paintings, guidebooks, and music.

About 8.5 million people received jobs over the eight years that the WPA was in operation. By 1943, World War II had created enough jobs that the WPA was no longer needed. It was cut on June 30 of that year.

On July 5, 1935, the National Labor Relations Act took effect. A year before the act was signed, half a million laborers went on strike in various industries. To provide for greater stability in businesses across the nation, the act created the National Labor Relations Board.

The board's job was to help employee groups decide if a labor union should represent their concerns. It was also supposed to prevent employers, employees, and unions from engaging in unfair labor practices.

Not everyone agreed with the National Labor Relations Act. But many labor unions showed their appreciation for it by strongly supporting Roosevelt in the 1936 presidential election.

Roosevelt signed the Social Security Act on August 14, 1935. Taxes were collected from businesses and employees and put into a special fund. The government used this money to provide a modest income to the elderly, to the sick, and to dependent children.

Just nine days later, Congress passed the Banking Act of 1935. It held banks more accountable to depositors. The Federal Deposit Insurance Corporation was also made permanent. This made the FDIC more powerful.

In 1938, Congress passed the Fair Labor Standards Act. This is sometimes also called the Wages and Hours Act. It was the last act of the New Deal.

The Fair Labor Standards Act set a minimum wage of 25¢ an hour, as well as a workweek of no more than 44 hours. Under this act, employers were required to pay employees extra money for working overtime. The act also made it illegal to buy and sell products between states that were made by children under a certain age.

A young girl tends a spinning machine at a cotton mill in North Carolina. Children worked the same hours as adults for poor wages until the reforms of the Fair Labor Standards Act of 1938.

A government poster encourages the public to apply for Social Security benefits.

A CHANGED NATION

Roosevelt's focus shifted away from issues within the United States in January 1939. Trouble was brewing in Europe. Roosevelt called for peace on April 14, but it was not to be. In September 1939, Adolf Hitler's army invaded Poland, and World War II began.

The United States joined in the fighting in 1941. The U.S. government had to spend a great amount on the military. Factories were flooded with orders for products needed to support the war. In fact, demand was so high that the shortage of jobs turned into a shortage of workers! Many historians think that the U.S. involvement in World War II did more to end the Great Depression than the New Deal legislation did.

Adolf Hitler

But even if the New Deal did not end the Great Depression, it still helped make many important changes. The legislation passed during the New Deal restored U.S. citizens' confidence in the government and changed the way the U.S. government operated.

Despite these successes, the New Deal had its critics. Some U.S. citizens felt that the New Deal legislation made people too dependent on government help. Other critics felt that Roosevelt's New Deal was not far reaching enough. They thought that the WPA jobs paid too little and helped too few unemployed people.

But Roosevelt's New Deal will long be remembered for the hope it brought to the American people. It started a movement toward a more active and inventive executive branch of government. The New Deal also helped give union members a stronger voice in politics. New avenues opened up for interest groups, and the Democratic Party became more solid.

During the Great Depression, people looked to the central government rather than to state governments for economic aid for the first time. This ushered in the era of strong central government that we are in today.

FRANKLIN D. ROOSEVELT

Franklin D. Roosevelt was the only U.S. president to serve three consecutive terms in office. He died early in his fourth term, on April 12, 1945, after serving more than 12 years.

In 1951, Congress passed the Twenty-second Amendment, which limits a president to two consecutive terms.

Franklin D. Roosevelt

TIMELINE

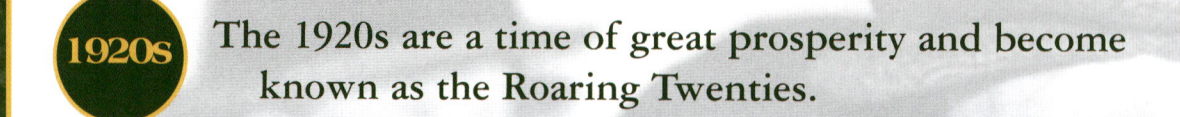

1918 — World War I ends.

1920s — The 1920s are a time of great prosperity and become known as the Roaring Twenties.

1928 and 1929 — The Federal Reserve Board raises interest rates on loans, causing a drop in consumer spending.

1929 — On October 24, share prices plunge. This day becomes known as Black Thursday.

On October 29, the U.S. stock market collapses. This day becomes known as Black Tuesday.

1930 — U.S. president Herbert Hoover signs the Hawley-Smoot Tariff Act in a failed effort to save the U.S. economy.

1932 — Franklin D. Roosevelt defeats Hoover in the U.S. presidential election.

1933   On March 6, President Roosevelt announces a bank holiday. This is his first initiative as president.

On March 9, Congress begins the Hundred Days.

On June 16, many important pieces of the New Deal legislation become law.

1935   On January 17, Roosevelt announces his plans for America's future to Congress. This begins the "second New Deal."

1939   In September, Hitler's army invades Poland, which begins World War II.

1941   The United States joins in the fighting of World War II after Pearl Harbor is bombed. Because of increased military production, the Great Depression ends.

American Moments

FAST FACTS

Not everyone enjoyed the prosperity of the 1920s. African Americans and farmers actually had a hard time economically.

Many U.S. citizens blamed President Herbert Hoover for the economic hardships of the Great Depression. Makeshift communities of homeless people were called "Hoovervilles."

In the 1920s, the overplanting of certain kinds of crops exhausted the nutrients in the soil. This led to severe wind erosion, which caused the Dust Bowl. After the Great Depression, crop rotation became more widely used to help avoid this problem.

President Franklin Roosevelt depended on advice from his "brain trust" for many of the policies he drafted. The brain trust consisted of professors and other academics.

Some upper-class people criticized Roosevelt for his policies. They felt that he had turned against the class to which he belonged by giving money to the poor at the expense of the rich.

Roosevelt delivered several "fireside chats" on the radio. He used them to communicate directly with the public. During the chats, he encouraged people to help each other through the economic crisis. The fireside chats made Roosevelt very popular.

WEB SITES
WWW.ABDOPUB.COM

Would you like to learn more about the Great Depression? Please visit **www.abdopub.com** to find up-to-date Web site links about the Great Depression and other American moments. These links are routinely monitored and updated to provide the most current information available.

Bankrupt investor Walter Thornton tries to sell his luxury roadster for $100 on the street after the 1929 stock market crash.

GLOSSARY

assembly line: a way of making a product where the equipment and workers are in a line. Each worker does a specific job along the line.

brokerage: a company that buys and sells stock. People usually buy stock through brokerages.

Federal Reserve Board: the board that oversees the well-being of the U.S. economy. One of the board's duties is to regulate interest rates.

labor union: a group formed to help workers receive their rights.

laissez-faire: free enterprise. It is the idea that business should regulate itself, free of government control. The French phrase means "leave alone."

malnutrition: not getting enough essential food elements such as vitamins and minerals to keep one's body healthy.

moratorium: a legally allowed delay in the repayment of debt.

overtime: working more hours than the set number of hours one is supposed to work. Employers usually pay an employee more money per hour for overtime.

unemployment: the state of being without a job. It is also the number of people in a country who do not have jobs.

World War I: from 1914 to 1918, fought in Europe. The United States, France, Great Britain, Russia, and their allies were on one side. Germany, Austria-Hungary, and their allies were on the other side. The war began when Archduke Ferdinand of Austria was assassinated. The United States joined the war in 1917 because Germany began attacking ships that weren't involved in the war.

World War II: from 1939 to 1945, fought in Europe, Asia, and Africa. The United States, France, Great Britain, the Soviet Union, and their allies were on one side. Germany, Italy, Japan, and their allies were on the other side. The war began when Germany invaded Poland. The United States entered the war in 1941 after Japan bombed Pearl Harbor, Hawaii.

INDEX

A
Agricultural Adjustment Act (AAA) 33, 34
B
Banking Act of 1935 37, 38
Black Thursday 16
Black Tuesday 18
C
Civilian Conservation Corps (CCC) 33, 34
Congress, U.S. 27, 30, 32–34, 37, 38
D
Democratic Party 30, 41
Dust Bowl 22
E
Emergency Banking Bill of 1933 32
Emergency Relief Appropriation Act 37
Europe 26–28, 40
F
Fair Labor Standards Act 38
Federal Deposit Insurance Corporation (FDIC) 32, 38
Federal Reserve Board 16

G
Germany 27
Glass-Steagall Act 32
Great Plains 22
H
Hawley-Smoot Tariff Act 27
Hitler, Adolph 40
Hoover, Herbert 27, 30, 31
Hoover Moratorium 27, 28
Hundred Days, the 33, 34, 36
N
National Industrial Recovery Act (NIRA) 33, 34
National Labor Relations Act 37
National Labor Relations Board 37
National Recovery Administration (NRA) 34, 36
New Deal 31, 33, 36–38, 40, 41
P
Poland 40

R
Reforestation Relief Act 34
Roaring Twenties 12–14, 26
Roosevelt, Franklin D. 30–33, 37, 38, 40, 41
S
second New Deal 37
Securities and Exchange Commission (SEC) 36
Securities Exchange Act of 1934 36
Social Security Act 37, 38
T
Tennessee Valley Authority (TVA) 33, 34
Treasury, Department of the 32
W
Works Progress Administration (WPA) 37, 41
World War I 12, 26
World War II 37, 40